D0190808

Leading Teams

Pocket Mentor Series

The *Pocket Mentor* Series offers immediate solutions to common challenges managers face on the job every day. Each book in the series is packed with handy tools, self-tests, and real-life examples to help you identify your strengths and weaknesses and hone critical skills. Whether you're at your desk, in a meeting, or on the road, these portable guides enable you to tackle the daily demands of your work with greater speed, savvy, and effectiveness.

Books in the series:
Leading Teams
Running Meetings
Managing Time
Managing Projects

Leading
Teams

Expert Solutions
to Everyday Challenges

Harvard Business School Publishing

Boston, Massachusetts

Copyright 2006 Harvard Business School Publishing Corporation

All rights reserved

Printed in the United States of America

10 09 08 07 06 05   5 4 3 2 1

No part of this publication may be reproduced, stored in or introduced into a retrieval system, or transmitted, in any form, or by any means (electronic, mechanical, photocopying, recording, or otherwise), without the prior permission of the publisher. Requests for permission should be directed to permissions@hbsp.harvard.edu, or mailed to Permissions, Harvard Business School Publishing, 60 Harvard Way, Boston, Massachusetts 02163.

Library of Congress Cataloging-in-Publication Data

Leading teams : pocket mentor.
    p. cm. — (Pocket mentor series)
  ISBN 1-4221-0184-3
  1. Teams in the workplace—Management. I. Series.
  HD66.L436 2006
  658.4'022—dc22   2006001213

The paper used in this publication meets the requirements of the American National Standard for Permanence of Paper for Publications and Documents in Libraries and Archives Z39.48-1992.

Contents

Mentor's Message: Juggling Managing and Leading   ix

Team Management: The Basics   1

What Is a Team?   3

A general overview of team definitions, types, benefits, and problems.

Identify the types of "teams"   4

Consider the benefits of teams   5

Understand the problems of teams   6

How to Plan for a Productive Team   9

Understand what teams do, what distinguishes productive teams, and how to set up your team for success.

Understand what teams do   10

Identify the characteristics of productive teams   12

Plan for your own productive team   14

Watch for signs of failure   16

How to Form a Productive Team   19

Select the people with the right skills, experience, and attitude. Appeal to each person's underlying motivations.

Identify team roles   20

Select the right kind of team members   20

How to Lead a Team   29

Understand the stages of the team process. Establish the team leader role as initiator, coach, and model.

Recognize the team process   30

Organize a start-up meeting   30

Make the team goals clear to every team member   32

Establish ground rules   33

Assume your role as leader   36

Improve team communication   38

Develop a high-performing team.   43

Take a periodic time-out   49

How to Handle Team Problems   51

Recognize problems early and deal with them effectively—from leadership mistakes to interpersonal conflicts that may threaten the team and its mission.

Keep the team on target   52

Examine your own leadership style   55

Deal with performance problems   55

Manage conflicts   57

Reunite factions   60

Step between one-on-one conflicts   62

Reinvigorate commitment   64

How to Evaluate Performance   69

Measures of success depend on both the team goals and team
performance.

Use appropriate performance measures   70

Select evaluation methods   72

Review the performance of individual team members   73

Reward your team   73

Tips and Tools   75

Tools for Leading a Team   77

Worksheets to help you plan, lead, and evaluate a team.

Test Yourself   87

A helpful review of the concepts presented in this guide. Take it before
and after you've read through the guide to see how much you've learned.

To Learn More   93

Further titles of articles and books if you want to go
more deeply into the topic.

Sources for Leading Teams   99

Notes   101

For you to use as ideas come to mind.

Mentor's Message: Juggling Managing and Leading

You've sat through many a team event grinding your teeth, thinking, *"It's time to move on"* or *"I wish he'd just make a decision."* Now it's finally your turn to lead the team, your opportunity to have a significant impact on the organization. How are you going to shape this group of individuals into the high-performing team you always dreamed of? What are you going to do? Suddenly, leading the team doesn't seem so easy.

In exercises, when I ask people to write down words that reflect their experiences on teams, among the first few are usually "frustration," "conflict," and "hidden agendas." But these are typically followed by "accomplishment," "shared victory," "fun," and even "exhilaration." The team can be an oasis of excitement, focused energy, and peak performance, or it can feel like an endless desert. What makes the difference?

Well, it's not rocket science. Almost anyone can lead a team effectively. What you need is a clear understanding of how teams work (and how they differ from individuals); a commitment to coordinating the details; empathy, patience, and persistence; and a few techniques for getting beyond the predictable hurdles.

This guide will provide you the first and last of these and may even help you see how and where to use your emotional intelligence in the team context. Before you dive in, I'd like to highlight a few of the key things to understand about leading teams.

First of all, as the team leader, you need to juggle two very different kinds of responsibilities: you have to manage and you have to lead. By *managing,* I mean coordinating, measuring, and driving the team's efforts—keeping their eyes on the ball when necessary, and on the clock and scoreboard when that's important. People don't like having their time wasted, so you need to make it easy for team members to give you their best effort. Good team management reassures and motivates team members—it demonstrates that it's worthwhile for them to commit to this effort.

But managing is not the same as leading. *Leading* is about guiding people. It is about listening, observing, and influencing individuals and the team's dynamics. It involves making team members feel valued, orchestrating participation, and shaping the team's perceptions of what they are doing together and why. Leading is motivating the team to persist through conflict and confusion to meet its higher purpose. It is about making appropriate interventions to get a team back on track.

In addition to managing and leading, many team leaders are also juggling a third major responsibility—that of content expert. One of the biggest challenges that team leaders face is how to contribute their expertise without letting their own perspective and interests dominate the team's agenda. When this happens, you will see other team members slowly withdraw their efforts. So be careful with this occasionally tricky responsibility.

A common misconception people have about teams is assuming that the negative contributions they observe (whether sins of omission or commission) are due to the flawed personality of one team member. Sometimes this is true, but far more commonly, team members' behavior is driven by their organizational roles and responsibilities. So a key part of leading a team is understanding those roles and figuring out how to help team members see how the demands of those roles (as well as their individual interests) can be met by contributing effectively to the team.

Also, keep in mind that teams are designed to create one product from the efforts of many. Don't let your team believe that merely "dividing the labor" without having a plan or sufficient time to *integrate* their work will produce the desired results. As the leader, always focus on how team members' efforts and knowledge can and will be integrated into a successful conclusion.

Finally, as a team leader, remember to enjoy the communal fun and the exhilaration of shared victories!

Anne Donnellon, Mentor

Anne Donnellon is an associate professor at Babson College in Wellesley, Massachusetts, where she teaches cross-functional teamwork, negotiation, and organizational design in the M.B.A. and executive education programs. The author of *Team Talk: The Power of Language in Team Dynamics* (Harvard Business School Press, 1996) and other training materials, she brings her considerable experience and sound advice to this topic.

Team Management: The Basics

What Is a Team?

> *"People acting together as a group can accomplish things that no individual acting alone could ever hope to bring about."*
> —Franklin Delano Roosevelt

A team can certainly be described as a group of people organized to work together, or a group who do similar work or who report to the same person. But the kind of team you will be leading is much more than these brief descriptions.

Identify the types of "teams"

Teams are not all alike when it comes to their design or their demands on team members. To make things a bit more complicated, not every "team" is really a team, and some groups that are called by other names occasionally do phenomenal teamwork. The chart on the next page is a short list of some of the many versions of teams out there in organizations.

As you can see, a functional team may be just a group of individuals who meet periodically but who are not integrated into a team structure. On the other hand, a tiger team or a task force fits the definition of a high-performing team with collaborative activities and a shared goal.

Functional team	An organizational group that reports to a single boss and that may or may not have to work together to meet the group's goals
Cross-functional team	A group made up of team members from different functions across the organization whose time is dedicated partially to the team's efforts and partially to other functional responsibilities
Tiger team	A group made up of team members from different functions across the organization whose time is totally dedicated to the team's efforts
Ad-hoc team or task force	A temporary group put together to solve a particular problem or explore a particular opportunity
Committee	An ongoing group that develops and monitors a particular philosophy, policy, or set of practices

HIGH-PERFORMING TEAM *n* **1:** a group of people with complementary skills who interact to achieve a common objective **2:** a group of people committed to a common purpose, common performance goals, and an approach for which they hold themselves collectively responsible.

Consider the benefits of teams

As Roosevelt wisely observed, a team can often outperform an individual. When teams work well, the results can be extremely powerful. Synergy created by members' diverse skills, experiences, and motivations enables teams to respond more quickly to technological, economic, and market changes in our increasingly complex world. An effective team can make better decisions, move more quickly, and solve problems more creatively than any group of talented people working independently. And of course many people enjoy, and are motivated by, working in teams—as a result, they deliver their best performance.

Thus, the many benefits of forming a team include:

- improved performance through a broader knowledge and experience base

- greater creativity, wider perspective, and increased effectiveness in tackling problems

- a willingness to respond to changes and take on risk

- a shared responsibility for assignments and a shared commitment to goals

- a more effective delegation of tasks

- a more stimulating and motivating environment for team members

Understand the problems of teams

Given certain problems or issues, creating a team may not provide the best solution. Why? Teams don't always function smoothly. In some situations, it is actually better to work alone. As the person responsible, you need to be aware of the potential pitfalls of team leadership. The most common problems are (1) team goals are unclear or conflicting, (2) people don't work well together, and (3) leading a team takes time.

When you plan on using a team, think about some of the possible difficulties as well as the benefits:

- conflicts among team members, caused by various human feelings and responses

- interference with an individual's expertise. The team process may actually diminish a team member's ability to produce.

- time and energy spent on developing a team community

- possible slowdown of decision making

- domination by one group or faction within the team of the other members, reducing the value of the whole team's contributions

"There are a few hallmarks of dysfunctional teams, as I've seen over the years. You see individuals pursing their own agendas as opposed to team agendas, unclear goals or goals that are not supported by the senior management, people who are unskilled or unsuited for teamwork, poor leadership, and/or lack of process. And you can see all these things in Dilbert.*"*
—Steve Sullivan,
     vice president for communications

As team leader, you will need to factor in these negative aspects to make sure you achieve the power of team productivity.

How to Plan for a Productive Team

"The crucial role of language
in human evolution was not the ability
to exchange ideas, but the increased ability to cooperate."
—Fritjof Capra

B efore you begin assembling your own team or shaping an inherited team, plan for the process by understanding those common features of teams that determine success or failure.

Understand what teams do

Even though a team's particular mission and goals will drive the activities it performs, any team's work tends to follow a typical pattern.

The team will

- clarify and commit to goals

- agree on an approach to the project

- develop a process to complete the tasks

- cross-train members

- execute the process

- evaluate and self-correct the process, depending on the results of measurement and analysis

- communicate with all parties involved.

Identify the team's purpose. A team is formed for a reason. Every member of the team has to know and understand the team's purpose and goals.

For example, will your team make a policy recommendation or will it implement a strategic plan? Will it solve a quality problem or work on a long-term basis? Will it develop a new product or handle the needs of an immediate crisis?

Whatever the mission, you as the team leader will redirect the team to its purpose again and again.

Recognize the scope of the team's activity. Teams often have sole authority over decisions related to team operations and processes, but upper management still has to approve and support the team's activities. For example, a team may make resource decisions but within senior-management-determined budget limitations.

As team leader, you and your supervisors need to have a shared vision of the team's purpose, as well as agreement in the following areas:

- personnel decisions, particularly on cross-functional teams

- expenditures beyond the budgeted level

- contracting with outside experts or consultants, or acquiring additional resources

- changes in the team's deliverables and schedule

Be sure that all members of your team and upper management understand and agree to the scope of the team's activities, particularly

- what decisions the team can make
- which decisions will be made outside the group
- how and when those decisions will be communicated to all involved.

Identify the characteristics of productive teams

As you plan, consider the predictable characteristics of productive teams. After all, you will be responsible for ensuring that these qualities become realities in your own team.

Within the most productive teams,

- members agree with the goals and are committed to them. If possible, the team members participate in setting realistic, specific goals.
- team goals are more important than individual goals.
- members clearly understand their roles and shift responsibilities as needed.
- members contribute a diverse, yet appropriate, mix of skills and experiences.
- members are tolerant of mistakes—their own and others'.
- members are open to new ideas, other perspectives, and risk taking.
- decisions are made on the basis of substance, not by the style or status of the individual proposing the idea.

Worksheet for Forming a Team

Team Purpose
Redesign bank Web site and put it online.

Expected Activities
Create new graphic look for all screens, update database and forms, update content from all banking areas.

Intended Results
More functional and user-friendly Web site for online banking customers that complies with security and legal guidelines.

Available Resources
Budget is approved; vendor has been selected and contract signed; ongoing support from technology department.

Constraints
Must coincide with new marketing efforts to launch in June; investment division is reorganizing—may be difficult to get timely feedback.

Necessary Skills and Qualities
Webmaster, approved input from each division of bank.

Expected Team Members

Extent of Decision-Making Authority (for example, Recommend or Implement)
Implement Web site.

Duration
7 months

To develop a productive team clearly takes plenty of people skills—communication, understanding, negotiating, and patience! Here's a tool for planning your team to fit your project needs.

Plan for your own productive team

NOTE: Steve Sullivan's recipe for creating a good team.

1. Common sense and good human behavior—50%
2. Shared desire for a positive outcome—20%
3. Clear process—20%
4. Content knowledge—10%

Mix together and knead into a successful team. Notice that content knowledge is part of the recipe, not what drives it.

Establishing a highly productive team takes effort on your part. It's a complex process that needs constant tending to. But, of course, it's worth it!

Set your team up for success. As a team leader, you are the liaison between your group and upper management or a client. Before you begin, set your team up for success. Carefully examine all the assumptions upper management or the client has made.

For example,

- Is the team's purpose clear?

- Are the budgets and deadlines realistic?

- Are the resources adequate for what you need to accomplish?

- Does the team have the authority and support it needs to get the job done?

If you answer *"no"* to any of these questions, you may need to push back—argue for your team and the reality of achieving its goals.

Be proactive. Be creative. *Pushing back* does not mean whining, complaining, or refusing to accept the job until all the stars are in alignment. Part of leading a team means taking the initiative. You can't expect everything you need to be placed in front of you at the outset, especially if you're new to team leadership and don't have much of a track record.

If you're short on resources,

- work your network. Get ideas and help from any appropriate person you can think of.

- call in favors from other people and departments.

- use your own initiative to find the people, equipment, and technology you need to make your job happen.

If time frames or budgets are completely unrealistic,

- propose realistic alternatives.

- make a strong case for what you need and why you need it.

- prove your need for more resources.

- demonstrate what *can* be done within the proposed amount of time or amount of money.

Pushing back requires political savvy and a careful use of influence. But every time you lead a team successfully, you improve your track record and your reputation. You will become increasingly able to attract the people you want on your team, and you can go after the projects you want to work on.

Be realistic. If you're *sure* the time frame is ridiculous or the resources simply aren't there, but you end up saying you can do it and hoping for the best, you've doomed your own team—and, perhaps, your professional career. Wishful thinking can only lead to disappointment and possible disaster. You lose credibility not only with upper management, but with team members and peers for bringing them onto a losing project. So be realistic—if the team's goals simply cannot be achieved given the constraints, don't get involved!

Watch for signs of failure

Teams can fail in many ways. Recognizing paths to failure is the first step to making sure your team doesn't make the wrong turn.

Why teams fail:

- lack of management support

- inadequate resources

- weak leadership (your role!)

- misunderstood or conflicting team goals

- limiting team focus to tasks, ignoring interpersonal relationships

- team members who do not take responsibility for themselves

- too many or too few team members

- lack of sense of interdependency and common vision

- inadequate reward systems

Careful planning can help you prepare your team for success on all levels.

How to Form
a Productive Team

Sometimes a team leader has the opportunity to assemble a complete team. But even the team leader of an ongoing or inherited team can still influence the personnel to some degree—for instance, by replacing someone who leaves, shifting responsibilities from one member to another, or using influence to increase staff.

Identify team roles

Even though different teams will have different skill requirements, every team needs a few predictable roles to be filled and shared. As you form your team, keep the roles in the following chart in mind.

Some of these roles overlap, and often they can be rotated so that team members can serve in different roles, gaining new experiences and spreading the duties around. Some types of teams may have shared leadership, especially self-directed teams.

Select the right kind of team members

When choosing team members, try to ensure that you recruit individuals who can contribute a complementary mix of skill sets. Look not only for those people who currently possess the skills the team needs, but also for those who have the potential to develop needed skills. While the ideal mix will vary depending on the team's mission, all teams require a blend of technical/functional expertise that includes the following:

- problem-solving and decision-making talents

- interpersonal skills

- team skills

"I look for a positive personality, someone who's flexible, open-minded, smart, and innovative. And someone who can check their ego at the door, someone who's willing to play their role, be a team player. You can get a smart, creative person who doesn't see he's operating as part of a team. I look for attitude. You can teach the skills to anyone who's intelligent."
   —Jeanne Weldon, event planner and former catering
      and conventions manager

Hire for attitude; train for skills. Of course, participants on a team need certain skills, but some managers focus exclusively on seeking the right skills, experience, and knowledge. Successful team leaders will tell you that attitude is just as important as skills and experience, even in jobs where great skill or knowledge is required.

How big should a team be? There is a natural tendency to let teams get too big—for a good reason. The leader wants everyone who is affected by the outcome of the team's work to be involved in the process. However if there are too many people on a team, productivity and effectiveness will suffer.

What Would YOU Do?

The Superstar

Matthew wanted to recruit the most talented people for the exciting account his agency had just landed. He was torn between the top contenders for art director: Marcia and Warren. Marcia hadn't worked on the pitch, but she was pushing for the job. Marcia had experience, numerous awards, and incredible talent. Her portfolio would bring prestige to the project. But every time he thought about working with her, he felt uncomfortable. She was great with the client, but she was such a prima donna behind the scenes! Part of him didn't feel like handling such a high-maintenance performer. Then there was Warren. Warren had worked on the pitch, but he had less experience than Marcia, no awards—at least not yet—and he lacked clout in the agency. Matthew knew it would be more fair—and more fun—to assign Warren to the job, even at the risk of annoying Marcia. But Marcia was a superstar. With her on board, the campaign stood a chance of winning a Clio!

What would YOU do? The mentor will suggest a solution in *What You COULD Do.*

TEAM ROLE	DUTIES
Team leader	• uses team to achieve goals • understands whole project • oversees process • guides without dominating • supports team and team members • helps team achieve productive working relationships
Team advisor	• champions the team within the organization • communicates with stakeholders
Facilitator	• schedules and conducts team meetings and other activities • serves as a resource person • encourages full participation
Process observers or team members	• support the leader and facilitator in promoting team culture • focus energy on tasks • listen to everyone's ideas
Scribe or recorder	• keeps written records of team meetings

Recruit team members. Members who voluntarily sign up for a team tend to bring far more commitment to the team than people who are assigned to work on it. Commitment is even stronger when people recognize that there is a very significant purpose behind the team effort. With a clear strategic focus, you will find it easier to recruit the team members you want.

Tip: Tips for Selecting Team Members

- Recruit individuals who can contribute a complementary mix of skill sets (project management expertise, financial skills).

- Select individuals with specific problem-solving and decision-making talents.

- Ask for recommendations from your manager and your colleagues.

- Look for individuals who have had team experience.

- Find people who will view this as an opportunity to combine skills and talents with others.

Tip: Tips for Establishing Team Size

- Use a small team (five to nine members) when tasks are complex and require specific skills.

- Use larger teams (up to 25 people) when the tasks are fairly simple and straightforward.

- Break large teams into subgroups if team members agree to delegate tasks as needed.

- Include an odd number of people on the team to facilitate decision making, since "majority rules" votes will never end in ties.

"If you put together a team inside an insurance company, you'll have the skills you need. The real important thing becomes attitude. I would say that attitude is 90 percent of it. If somebody has the right attitude—they're enthusiastic, they work hard, and they want something to happen as a result of a project as opposed to just wanting the project to end—if they've got those three things going for them, they can learn most anything they need to know."
—Steve Sullivan

Be sensitive to people's motivations. Everyone coming to a team brings talents, reservations, interests, and motivations. The art of recruiting involves understanding people's needs and desires and working to meet them.

What typically motivates people? Not necessarily money.

For example, people may want

- the chance to learn and grow professionally
- recognition for creative accomplishments
- the pleasure of the team affiliation and working with others.

"New team members arrive not only with the required skills, but also with a legacy of skepticism."
—Anne Donnellon

Be clear about contributions and rewards. Be sure that team members know how their contributions will lead to their rewards. Even if you are not recruiting a new member, you can convert a less-than-enthusiastic member by responding to his potential personal or professional desires.

Tip: Tips for Handling Virtual Teams

Today, people want to travel less, yet for many teams travel is a way of life. When you minimize travel for road-weary team members, your team becomes more productive.

- Encourage team members who want to reduce travel to improve methods of "virtual" communication.
- Establish agreements as to how, when, and how often you are going to communicate with one another—virtually or in person.
- Schedule meetings carefully. When creating schedules, analyze how much travel is *really* necessary. A kick-off meeting, for example, is important, but other meetings could be managed virtually.
- Communicate with your team members frequently— daily if possible.
- Assess and use technology wisely. Get high-quality speakerphones. Consider videoconferencing, either by setting up a system in-house or by using local video-conferencing services. Web conferencing and virtual private networks (VPNs) are other technologies that can reduce travel time.

Source: *Inc. Magazine*, January 2002

What You COULD Do.

Let's go back to Matthew's problem.

The mentor suggests this solution:

This example touches on a common problem a lot of team leaders face—dealing with a big ego. Some managers feel personally threatened by characters like Marcia. But this is Matthew's problem, not Marcia's. Matt may have to manage Marcia individually while managing the team. My first reaction is to ask, why not use both Warren and Marcia? Marcia, being more experienced, can help Warren develop. Matthew can involve Marcia in the team process by involving her as a mentor to Warren. You should always keep fairness in mind, but getting the job done is important, and Marcia brings talent and experience. So I would suggest to Matthew that the ideal solution is to find a way to get them to work well together in the interest of the project.

Teams that take the individual needs of people into account do a better job than teams that just focus on skills. Is someone hesitant to join the team because your culture may demand a 70-hour work week? If that person's knowledge and expertise are valuable to your team, can you negotiate a relationship that assures him that he won't be working until 9:00 every night? Is there some way to measure his contribution other than by the number of hours he puts in?

What opportunities for growth, creativity, advancement, and excitement can you offer the people you are trying to recruit? Negotiate as creatively as possible, but remember to deliver whatever you promise.

How to Lead
a Team

The role of team leader may start with identifying the original mission, planning the project, and choosing the team members, but the real work begins now. The team comes together as a cluster of separate people gathered in one room, and you have to begin shaping these individuals into a cohesive team committed to a shared mission.

Recognize the team process

The team leader needs to anticipate and be ready for an interpersonal group process that is natural and predictable. Teams go through different stages of development, which often include times of tension and conflict, before the team settles down to its own peculiar style of working together.

Expect the following human responses during the course of the team's life span.

The team leader guides the team through these phases because managing group process is as important to achieving the team goal as the task content.

Organize a start-up meeting

Whether you are beginning a project with a new team or an inherited one, a start-up or kick-off meeting can set the scene for all involved.

PHASE	RESPONSES
Team formation	Excitement, high expectations, establishing roles and rules
Team conflict	Competition among team members, confusion about roles and tasks, discouragement, conflict
Team normalization	Team routines settled, teamwork forms, trust evolves
Team performance	Hopefulness, productiveness, shared leadership

What is on the agenda for the start-up meeting? Common items are as follows:

- Introduce team members to one another. Ask each person to say something about himself or herself (for example, name, department, expertise, role on team).

- Explain clearly to everyone the purpose of the team. What are its goals? What does it have to accomplish? Within what time frame? Gain agreement or alter the expectations.

- Establish team ground rules about how the team will operate. How will decisions be made? How will meetings be run?

- Begin the process of instilling a sense of mission and cohesiveness in your team. That feeling has to come from your own enthusiasm about the team's mission.

What Would YOU Do?

The Team That Wouldn't Grow Up

U pper management had made it clear to Linda that her team's latest assignment was top priority, so she decided that they might as well get down to business. In her crisp, logical way, she explained to her team the work that lay ahead of them and emphasized their lack of choice in the matter. The tasks were pretty obvious, but she wanted to make sure that everyone was on the same page at the outset. Linda was annoyed when the discussion went into a tailspin. The group, normally a mature, level-headed crowd, insisted on searching for ways to avoid the assignment. They complained about the budget, the deadline, and the means of getting there. They knew that she had not asked for this assignment. Why couldn't they all just bite the bullet and get it over with?

What would YOU do? The mentor will suggest a solution in *What You COULD Do.*

Make the team goals clear to every team member

You've already determined the overall goals with senior management or your client. But now is the time to not only present the goals clearly to the group but also invite them to participate in the process of defining the goals more precisely or breaking the larger goal into smaller subgoals and performance milestones. Any way that you can help the group feel a part of the mission will begin the transformation of the group into a team.

See the *Checklist for Assessing Your Team's Goals* in the Tools section to help you and your team in the process of internalizing and championing the overall mission of the team.

Create an internal brand. It's good, but is it CHIFF? For some groups, marketing techniques can help create a team brand that keeps everyone focused on the mission. Ask members for adjectives that describe the team philosophy and purpose. Then create a mission statement that's easy to remember and that will always remind team members of their goal as they proceed. At Cranium, founding entrepreneurs coined the term CHIFF—Clever, High Quality, Innovative, Friendly, Fun—to describe everything their product would be.

"CHIFF means that our employees and partners will come to the same decisions that Whit and I would, without a lot of hand-holding. Meetings are faster and more efficient, even with foreign manufacturers, because we've created a common language."
—Richard Tait, former software developer at Microsoft and
co-founder of Cranium, a successful board game company

Establish ground rules

The most important ground rule is determining how decisions will be made. Team work typically requires constant decision making, and the more involved the all team members are in the decision-making process, the more likely it is that they will support the outcome.

Choose the decision-making processes your team will use. Decisions are typically made in a few basic ways:

1. **Leader decides with team input.** This may be the fastest method but the least likely to ensure full support of the team. If, however, team members feel their opinions have been heard and considered—and they trust the leader—this method may work well.

2. **Majority decides.** This method is a familiar and commonly accepted decision-making process; however, the losers often feel left out of the process.

3. **Small group of experts decides.** Again, trust becomes extremely important when using this method of making decisions.

4. **Decision by consensus.** Attaining a consensus does *not* mean that all members agree with the decision; rather, that all members can live with it. As a result, building consensus can help build team commitment. Part of being a team player means accepting the fact that you will have to support team decisions even when you may have reservations or when the decision isn't exactly what you would like. However, consensus building—unlike leader decides—is the slowest type of decision making—a problem when decisions must be made quickly.

Tip: Team leaders have to be able to subvert their egos but not their judgment.

There are variations on the decision-making process, but the one that has the most support from the team is usually the best.

"Typically a team at Liberty Mutual is put together to analyze an opportunity or problem and make a recommendation to someone more senior. There is a very clear rule going in that the team has to be rigorous about their data. If we're analyzing a marketing problem among agents, we have to talk to a credible cross-section of agents. The data will be geographically mixed and represent most of our lines of business. You don't vote on it. Those are facts. There's discussion about the data parameters, but at the end of the day, it's what will produce the most accurate picture of the data we're trying analyze."
—Steve Sullivan

Agree to other basic guidelines. Go over some other rules that will make your team work more smoothly through the process.

For example, have the team discuss and agree that:

- all meetings will start and stop on time

- each meeting will have an agenda

- all team members will attend and participate in team meetings

- all criticism must be constructive

- differences of opinion will be recognized and explored

- all members will keep others informed on a need-to-know basis, using the *Team Contact Information Form.*

By establishing these (or other) rules, you can avoid many problems in the future.

An example of a *Team Contact Information Form* can be found on the following page.

Assume your role as leader

Successful leaders and team players recognize that a team is interdependent. Relying on others is necessary for a team to be successful.

Successful leaders and team members have one thing in common: the ability to break out of their egos.

Play the team leader's roles. You are now in a position where your team members often have more expertise than you have in certain areas, so you can't always be the expert or even the problem-solver. Your roles may adapt to the team, but will quite likely continue to include the following.

- **Team leader as initiator.** You begin actions and processes that promote team development and performance.

- **Team leader as coach.** You serve as a counselor, mentor, and tutor to help team members improve their performance.

- **Team leader as model.** You shape your behavior and performance to reflect the expectations you have for your team.

- **Team leader as negotiator.** People on your team may have very different ways of thinking, doing things, relating to each other, and expressing their ideas. You need to be open to these differences—and recognize that these qualities can be difficult to

Team Contact Information

Use this form to record each team member's contact information,
including how and when he or she prefers to be reached.

TEAM MEMBER: Julia Trevisan			Role: Project Manager
Mailing Address: Springfield Trust, 89 Market St., Springfield, NA 99999			E-Mail: J_Trevisan@springbank.com
Office Phone Number	Home Phone Number	Fax Number	Best Time to Call
555-555-5555	505-555-8976	555-555-4321	mornings
TEAM MEMBER: Fan Wu			Role: Webmaster
Mailing Address: Springfield Trust, 89 Market St., Springfield, NA 99999			E-Mail: F_Wu@springbank.com
Office Phone Number	Home Phone Number	Fax Number	Best Time to Call
555-555-5544	555-234-0300	555-555-4321	Afternoons and evenings until 8:00
TEAM MEMBER: Sylvia Goncharev			Role: Producer
Mailing Address: Rare Media Designs			E-Mail: Sylvia@RareMedia.com
Office Phone Number	Home Phone Number	Fax Number	Best Time to Call
555-674-5000	505-555-7653	555-674-5244	All day

deal with but are what can make the team dynamic and effective. Negotiating these differences and drawing out the creativity from them is one of your most important roles.

"My participation in hockey had a profound impact on how I work with other people. When you're playing in a competitive sport, you know what's out there. You know the competition is real. So you have to break out of your ego. You're not the best player that ever was. There's a level of humility required to play a team sport effectively."

—Timothy O'Meara,
     director of technical services

Improve team communication

Communication is the key to keeping a team productive and functioning smoothly. You can get the most out of your team if you establish a formal routine for team dialogue.

Make sure roles and responsibilities are clear. Each team member needs to know not only his reason for being there but also how everyone else fits together to form the team. One way to discover misconceptions is to use a *Role Clarification Worksheet* tool. When you read how each team member perceives the others' positions and duties, you'll quickly see what you need to clarify, restate, or readjust.

Listen to your team. Start with yourself by listening carefully and remaining open-minded. Seek out team members' opinions and ideas and use them. When leaders consistently ignore the advice and input of team members, the whole team suffers.

The team leader who doesn't listen reduces the team's chances of winning and frustrates players who want to make valuable contributions. The leader who says *"this is how it's going to be"* makes it less likely that members will be motivated to contribute.

"Last week in Pittsburgh, something wasn't working, so we're talking about it on the sideline. They're asking us what we think 'Yeah, no, maybe,' but because we discussed it, everybody was of one accord when we went back on the field. That's much better than, 'We're going to run this regardless.'"

— Terrell Buckley, New England Patriots Defensive Back *(speaking after the Patriots upset the heavily favored Pittsburgh Steelers in the 2001 football playoffs)*

Role Clarification Worksheet

Ask each team member to complete the worksheet. Responses can be compared as part of a team discussion about roles.

1. List roles/responsibilities of each team member:

Team Member Name	Roles/Responsibilities
Julia	Project manager; oversee budget and schedule; supervise content delivery from Banking, Loans, and Investment groups to Web site producer; sign off on graphic design; oversee technical and security; clear documents through legal
Fan Wu	Work with web-site producer to develop technical requirements, implement new site on bank server; oversee security requirements; work with producer to train onsite technical staff; design database
David	Oversee development of employment opportunity section of site
Terry	Provide producer with approved content about consumer banking products
Juan	Provide and review content about consumer loans
Jessica	Provide and review content about commercial banking
Barton	Provide and review content about investment opportunities
Sasha	Review all design and content for consistency and style requirements

2. Roles or specific areas of responsibility that are unclear:

Aspects of my role that are unclear: Number of meetings I am expected to attend; number of people who will be trained

Aspects of others' roles that are unclear: Relationship with Sylvia—will my input and questions go through Julia, or will I be dealing directly with the vendor?

3. Roles that overlap or conflict: NA

On the other hand, the leader who values others' contributions inspires all team members to contribute at their highest level. Listening and responding to ideas becomes a cycle of success and reward. The act of using a team member's good ideas moves the team forward and rewards the individual and the team at the same time.

Tip: Tips for Building Team Performance

- Establish an urgent and worthwhile purpose and a clear direction.
- Select team members on the basis of their knowledge, experience, skills, and attitudes, not on their personalities.
- Be alert to what happens in the first few meetings, including actions taken.
- Set clear rules of behavior.
- Establish immediate performance-oriented tasks and goals.
- Keep providing new facts and information to create a challenge.
- Use positive feedback, recognition, and rewards to encourage team members.

Review the format for team discussion during meetings. Meetings, of course, provide the most open forum for team communication, so pay special attention to how the meetings will be structured.

Here are some guidelines that you might choose to adopt:

- Follow the same format for all team meetings so that members know what to expect from the gathering. This format becomes a habit for the team and often improves productivity at meetings.

- Familiarize yourself with the agenda before each meeting. It will help you be prepared for the ensuing debate.

- Focus on problem solving during the meeting instead of information sharing.

- Don't waste valuable meeting time on information that could be distributed ahead of time.

- Keep the discussion on track—when it strays, steer it back to items on the agenda.

- Suggest that new business be discussed at the end of the meeting.

Some of these tasks will be performed by a facilitator—you or another team member fulfilling that role.

Encourage all members to contribute by asking their opinions. At team meetings, ask each member explicitly what he or she thinks of a proposal so that everyone stays involved. Stop the free flow of conversation occasionally, go around the table, and give each member a turn to talk. Some members may be shy and hesitate before interrupting a heated debate to add their opinion. When you structure time for everyone to participate, the team will benefit from each member's opinion.

Deliberately examine opposing points of view. Opposing views and creative conflict can be a rich source for new ideas, but they need to be managed carefully. Encourage all points of view:

- Assign a team member to act as devil's advocate on all major debates and decisions. Even if the team seems to agree, it will force members to reexamine their views.

- Ask for all possibilities, and examine them. When only one solution is proposed, members may feel that their input isn't needed and the team may lose out on terrific alternatives.

- Ensure that all members have the opportunity to voice their opinions and offer their suggestions.

"You get people to feel as though they have a voice in the managing of the place. Really use their input and follow through on it. There's nothing more rewarding than someone thinking of a different way to achieve something and then hearing, 'Yeah, you're right.'"
—Jeanne Weldon

Encourage the team to talk often about its goals.

- Talking about goals will help ensure you're all working to accomplish the same thing.

- Revisit the initial purpose of the team periodically. When a project is under way, it's easy to get lost in the details.

- Write frequent progress reports to be distributed to all team members. Seeing the progress in writing will remind you of where you are and where you want to go.

"I frequently have to coach people on writing skills. The written document is so important as part of the group process—at the beginning and the end. And it's a skill that's in very short supply in business."
—Steve Sullivan

NOTE: Develop your writing skills. Why? Because a team leader has to communicate in writing for many reasons.

For example, team leaders

- write reports to senior management to show the team's progress
- make requests for additional resources in clearly written, persuasive documents
- report the final output of the team's work in a written report.

If your writing skills could use improvement, find a mentor to help you, take a class in business writing, or use a style guide or grammar book. If your writing skills are good, coach team members on their writing skills to enhance the performance of the entire group.

Develop a high-performing team

Simply put, the sooner you can get your team working together, instead of as individuals, the more productive that team will be.

"In the hotel, you'd have a room that was a conference room all day and at night there would be a banquet. We'd have very little time to make that change. We called it a "tight turn." Everyone—people from management, people from every department, people wearing high heels—everyone would all come flooding to the ballroom and start moving furniture and changing over the room. When you're working together like that, everyone is equal. And in twelve minutes, the chefs were coming in with their high hats on, putting chafing dishes on the table."
—Jeanne Weldon

Focus on collective performance. To help the group learn to operate as a team, focus on the team's overall performance. Whenever possible, give team members the opportunity to become active participants in the team's decision-making process. Empowerment fosters a working environment based on trust and collaboration.

Build collaboration out of conflict. Assume team members will encounter conflict, and assist them in working through to a productive result.

How? Here are a few ways to create collaboration out of conflict:

- Direct the team's process to stay focused on goals.

- Encourage the sharing of diverse ideas and opinions, and move the team toward general agreement.

- Show team members that by putting the team's interests ahead of their own, their career goals will benefit.

- Use reward systems that make team performance more valuable than individual performance.

A high-performing team executes the basics of teamwork and manages the dynamics deliberately. Just like the two sides of a ribbon, the basic mechanics and the dynamics are seamless, inseparable parts of good teamwork. See figure 1.

Keep the team focused and informed on its goals. Talking about goals will help ensure that you're all working to accomplish the same thing. Revisit the initial purpose of the team often. It's easy to get lost in the details, but you want to keep the team working together, moving toward its communal goal.

FIGURE 1

Strategies of high-performing teams

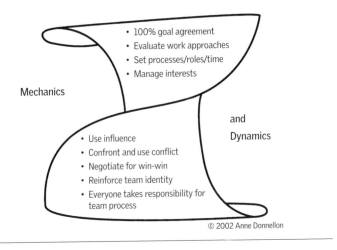

- 100% goal agreement
- Evaluate work approaches
- Set processes/roles/time
- Manage interests

Mechanics

and

Dynamics

- Use influence
- Confront and use conflict
- Negotiate for win-win
- Reinforce team identity
- Everyone takes responsibility for team process

© 2002 Anne Donnellon

Create a positive culture. A pleasant working environment is the most effective environment for a team to do its job. Establish an atmosphere in which everyone feels recognized and comfortable making contributions. Often this will require creativity on your part: an unsolicited letter to a person's superior, prominent mention in articles about the team, or time off for personal reasons.

"As a leader, you have to keep the focus on the team results and not your personality. A good team leader sets clear expectations—little things like, 'Okay, here are the five things we agreed on for today: Beth is gonna do this, Mark's gonna do that, and I'm gonna do

that.' *A leader has to take on some of the work himself. You can't delegate everything. A quarterback has to throw the ball. And you search for clarity at every step—clarity in what people are saying, what they're writing; clarity in final outcome, clarity in next steps. Search for clarity and you'll do well."*

—Steve Sullivan

Tip: Tips for Seeking Clarity

- Work with the group to establish immediate performance-oriented tasks and goals.
- Maintain an objective stance during any team conflict.
- Keep the group focused on an urgent and worthwhile purpose and a clear direction.
- Insist on polite and respectful behavior toward each other at all times.
- Use positive feedback, recognition, and rewards to keep the team moving forward.

"Making the money is great, but there are awards and then there are rewards. Our survival and success will come from optimizing fun, focus, passion, and profits. That takes smarts, and we thrive on that."

—Richard Tait

A supportive culture particularly helps team members who are struggling. Often, group members may feel embarrassed to ask for extra resources that they might need. It's your job as a leader to be sensitive to areas where people need development as team players and to coach them on how to get what they need.

"A woman was having difficulty learning the technical aspects of the software, but she had a good team leader. The team leader got the right person from IS and took her through a tutorial, but he did it in a way that didn't suggest to her that she was screwing up. [His attitude was] 'We need some more resource here, let's get it. She's putting in the hours, and the rest of her interaction with the team is dynamic, energetic, and committed.' *When someone is struggling with one aspect [of her job], you help [her]. . . . If a baseball player is having trouble with his hitting, you don't punish him; you put him into practice with the hitting coach."*

—Steve Sullivan

Empower your team. Give your team the authority it needs to participate in making decisions about how team goals will be achieved:

- Use consensus, as opposed to majority vote, to arrive at team decisions whenever possible.

- Encourage team members to solve problems that are within their realm of expertise.

- Keep an open mind in seeking out the opinions and ideas of team members.

- Provide positive reinforcement to team members for their participation.

Tip: Top Ten Team-Talk Tips

- Use "we" and "us" (when referring to team).
- Refer often to team goals and interests.
- Use questions to open space for dialogue.
- Don't interrupt low-power people.
- Say "I don't understand. Could you say it another way?"
- Ask "Can you tell me WHY that's important to you?"
- Ask "What are your reservations or concerns?"
- Ask "What are our options at this point?"
- Suggest "What if we . . . ?"
- Suggest "Let's stop for a minute and revisit our objectives (or examine the process)."

Model your own values. As a leader, make your values clear at the outset. Consistent values at the beginning and during the process will help create a healthy, compassionate environment.

"I have beliefs about how you should act as a teammate and how you should represent Brookline High School. I don't like trash talking, lack of sportsmanship. I want people to work the hardest they can, and I don't want them to get in trouble at school. I demand that. Or you don't play."

—Scott Ferguson, boys varsity soccer coach

Take a periodic time-out

The time-out process allows your team to step back from the daily tasks and observe how the team process is working. It can also serve as a reminder and refresher about where you've been and where you're going.

Use the following tool to gather information from each team member about how the team is doing as a whole. You'll be able to identify problem areas early enough to discuss them with the team and find ways to improve or resolve.

What You COULD Do.

What about Linda's problem?

The mentor suggests this solution:

If I were Linda, and my team was asked to do an unpleasant task, I would work with the team very early to get them to recognize that in every work environment there are things that no one wants to do, but someone has to do them. Linda can work with the team to figure out how to apply their talent and energy into minimizing the effort and maximizing the output. Linda should also negotiate with upper management for a better project next time around, and use the promise of a good future project to help motivate the team to get through the current one.

Team Time-Out: How Are We Doing?

Use this time-out audit periodically to gather information from each team member to create a group profile the team can use as a focal point for a discussion about, "How well are we doing as a team?" The discussion provides an opportunity to compare points of view objectively, and if need be, to get back on track and move forward more productively. Each team member can complete the time-out audit. Individual responses should be kept confidential. Compile the individual responses into a group profile for the team to share in a team meeting.

Team Name: Fan Wu   **Date:** 01/09/03

Team Goals/Team Purpose: Springfield Trust Web site Redesign

Rate your opinion of the team's effectiveness on the dimensions listed below, with "1" representing an ineffective area in need of improvement to "5" representing an area of effectiveness and strength.

Aspect/Dimension	1	2	3	4	5	Comments/Example
Goals/purpose					x	Clear goals
Meetings		x				Have to go to meetings where I don't need to be
Ground rules and norms				x		Team is usually respectful of each other
Communication			x			Not always sure of next step
Leadership (designated or rotating leadership)			x			Hectic and last-minute at times
Workload/distribution of work				x		Seems fair
Energy/commitment level				x		Good, people committed
Resources (availability/adequacy)			x			New site requires more tech staff
Management of stress				x		Seems ok
Decision making			x			Too much discussion, David obstructs progress
Respect for differences/diversity				x		David does not understand process well
Management of conflict			x			David keeps pushing his own ideas without listening
Level of participation/inclusion				x		David talks too much

Comments:

The biggest challenge we face as a team is: Getting this site up in time to coincide with new marketing campaign, especially if complicated ideas being pushed by David must be executed.

Our greatest strength as a team is: Respect and competence of most members

The one thing I would most like to see the team do is: Have fewer meetings

How to Handle
Team Problems

Keep the team on target

Teams can get sidetracked for a variety of reasons. Team members' sense of direction may weaken as a result of your leadership style, the team's internal working, or conflict within the team.

Find out what the problem is. As soon as you realize there's a problem, deal with it. The first step is to figure out what's wrong. The problem could be rooted in

- misunderstood, or ill-defined goals

- a lack of focus on team dynamics

- a lack of communication among team members

- insufficient or unequal commitment to the team's performance

- gaps in critical skills

- unresolved internal conflict

- external misunderstanding, hostility, or indifference from other groups.

Begin to resolve the problem. Don't avoid or deny it, hoping it will go away. Problems have a way of hanging around and growing larger if ignored.

There may be relatively simple things you can do to help a team get back on track.

For example:

- Lead a discussion that revisits the team's purpose, approach, and performance goals.

- Establish a common, immediate goal and achieve it.

- Bring in new information and different perspectives from within the organization.

- Share outside information or knowledge via benchmarks, case histories, and interviews.

- Use a facilitator to review your team process.

- Say "thank you" to your team members.

"The art of leading a team is to persuade a person who's unmotivated—and that can range from an attorney to a secretary—to do her job. If you haven't begun with a reasonable foundation for what you're doing, you won't get anywhere. You communicate the urgency, and the reasons. And always show appreciation. Thank people for opening a door, whether they do it figuratively or literally. 'Thank you for writing a nice piece of code; thank you for finding a legal document.' *Haven't you ever worked for someone who never says thank you? Every day of life is a punishment. There's no carrot; there's only stick. And that's an unpleasant way to live."*

—Timothy O'Meara

What Would YOU Do?

Bad Day at Black Rock

D erek and his team were pretty nervous when the beta left for the trade show with the Black Rock sales and marketing forces. Then, all that week, not a single call from Dallas. "They're busy; they're schmoozing; they're working 12-hour days; they're partying!" Everyone thought of good reasons why the phone didn't ring, but an ominous feeling began to creep over the group. The mood got darker with each passing day.

When the sales force returned on Monday, the team learned that its worst fears were nothing compared to the reality. Not only were the customers unimpressed, everyone else at the show was raving about their rival's beta—a real showstopper, they said! Derek's team was demoralized. How could they possibly move on to phase two when phase one was such a disaster? Although Derek was down himself, he knew he had to do something to keep the team from imploding. But what?

What would YOU do? The mentor will suggest a solution in *What You COULD Do.*

Examine your own leadership style

Before you start to analyze or critique your team, step back and take an honest, hard look at your own leadership style. Your behavior and attitudes may be causing, or at least exacerbating, the problem. Use the *Checklist for Evaluating Yourself as a Team Leader* Tool in the Tools section to discover where you may need to improve your leadership skills.

Find ways to improve your leadership. When your team sees you making an effort to change your ways, that may improve their attitudes, confidence, and productivity. Try some of these potential solutions:

- Revisit your weak areas (for example, confusion about goals or ground rules) and strengthen them through communication and repetition.

- Brainstorm alone or with colleagues for ideas on how to improve or how to get help.

- Talk with your supervisor.

- Ask your team members for their input.

Most importantly, put aside your ego and be honest with yourself.

Deal with performance problems

After you've examined the way you perform your *own* job, look closely at your team to determine what interpersonal problems may be contributing to the productivity problem. Typical issues include perceived or real inequities in skill levels, work levels, or compensation; interpersonal conflicts; or clash of personalities.

Turn an individual problem into a team contributor. Often, one team member seems to cause more trouble than all the others combined. That person could be viewed by the rest of the team as

- a slacker or "dead weight" who doesn't do his fair share of the work

- a mini-leader who tries to dominate the team

- a self-promoter who tries to take all the credit for the team's work

- a competitor who has to win in every situation

- a complainer who never sees the "job-well-done."

Do NOT pretend there isn't a problem! That response will only make things worse. Follow a problem-solving pattern to transform the problematic person into a real contributor. (See Steps sequence.)

For example, if a person is considered a dead weight, someone who's along for the ride who doesn't do much at all, other team members probably resent the fact—real or perceived—that she is not doing her job. How do you handle this situation before it becomes a major problem, slowing progress or souring the team culture?

Steps for Managing a Problem

1. Talk to the person privately. Let her know what the problem is and how people perceive her. Ask what she thinks about her work. Try to have her explain why she behaves in this way.

2. After the private talk, analyze why you think the person isn't doing the job. Is there some reason she feels that her contribution doesn't matter? Does she have the right skills for the job? Was she assigned to the team against her will?

3. If appropriate, privately query other team members to get their views about why this person is having problems. Don't ask for criticism, but for underlying reasons for the behavior.

4. If the solution is simple—she needs more training, for example—then act on it.

5. If necessary, talk to the person again to explain the urgency of the team goal and her important role in achieving that goal. Make clear why her contribution is important.

6. Give her positive feedback on her work.

7. If, however, the person's work and attitude does not improve, then consider removing her from the team.

Manage conflicts

Creative and intellectual conflict can be healthy. When members disagree about results, interpretations, approaches, and philosophies, and they argue their differences in a healthy, constructive way, they can produce extraordinary results.On the other hand, unmanaged conflict can undermine the team's effort and its shared goal.

Intervene quickly when necessary. When a creative conflict gets out of control or stuck, members start spinning their wheels. Act immediately by redirecting members back to the team goal. Ask them, *"What are we trying to accomplish?"*

If you can't seem to get the team moving again, agree on an objective third-party arbiter. Seek an expert opinion from someone outside the team or find data that resolves the issue. Or try testing an idea or prototype to stop a former disagreement from hindering progress.

"If we and our ad agency are really at loggerheads about a creative direction on an ad, we will market test it . . . but if there's ever a dispute, the tie goes to the consumer. And we both live by that. . . . There have [only] been a few instances, three in the last three years, and it either went our way or the agency's way based on input directly from the consumer. And we both are happy to live with that because it helps us move toward our goal."
—Steve Sullivan

Handle noncreative conflicts. Conflicts that are personal or are rooted in power plays have the potential to be far more destructive than creative conflicts. Your inability or unwillingness to address conflict openly can be one of the major roadblocks to team progress. If you sidestep an issue because you're worried about someone's feelings getting hurt, the team won't be able to move to the next task. The unresolved conflict will simply get worse, and could eventually shut down the team.

Working through a Disagreement

Use this worksheet to diagnose a disagreement among team members and to plan a discussion about how to "get unstuck."

Describe the disagreement. David wants to put up an 8-minute video about Springfield Bank to attract new employees and create an interactive form on site that would link to employment opportunities, but Fan does not want to implement or monitor the results from an additional form. Sylvia has pointed out that this is not in Rare Media's budget and would be an overage.

Diagnose the disagreement. *(Who is involved in the disagreement? What's the underlying cause? What's at stake for these team members?)* The goal of the team is to rebuild the online banking site to make online banking easier for our customers. While we have specified a section for employment opportunities, it is not the primary mission of this project.

Team Member	What's at Stake for This Team Member?
1. David	1. ownership of idea
2. Fan	2. technical requirements
3. Sylvia	3. concern with overage

What's at stake here for you? Keeping team on target; reaching consensus

What setting will you use for the discussion? After meeting privately with the individuals, I'll bring Fan, Sylvia, and David together in a meeting designed to finalize decisions about the recruitment section of the site.

Script a discussion about the disagreement. *(What do you plan to say? How might others respond?)*

What You Plan to Say	How Others May Respond
1. Set the stage; review purpose of site	1. Probably agreement
2. Mention proposed online video	2. Review pros & cons, tecinical issues
3. Explore alternatives, reach agreement	3. May suggest another option

Generate alternative solutions *(Team members should have an opportunity to offer possible solutions first. Generate a dialogue to explore solutions and why the topic is important.)*

Solutions	How/Why This Solution Adds Value
1. Shorten video to 1 min.	1. Adds interest but less technically demanding
2. Another alternative	2. Clarify value—get input

Discover the underlying cause of the conflict. You can't deal with a conflict unless you truly understand where it's coming from.

Is the conflict rooted in

- a creative disagreement?

- a lack of equality?

- a lack of understanding between two groups?

- a lack of appreciation?

- different personality styles?

- the unreasonable behavior of one individual?

- the incompetence or negligence of an individual?

- an unreasonable goal?

The problems could even be external or domestic problems expressing themselves inappropriately in the work setting.

If you can determine the real cause or root of the conflict, your chances of resolving it are much improved.

Here's a worksheet that can help you organize your thoughts before you begin the problem-solving process.

Reunite factions

A faction occurs when a subgroup splits off from the team as a whole. The subgroup tends to hold different philosophies or maintain different procedures than the team as a whole. Its unwillingness to negotiate or reach a consensus results in a fragmented and disabled team.

Fractious factions form when:

- Some people perceive themselves as smarter, more valuable, or better than others in any way.

- Reward systems are perceived as unequal.

- One group of people has more power (over resources or information, for example) than others.

- There is a powerful "old guard," a group who feel their seniority gives them special privileges.

- There are differences in tenure.

- Geographic distributions divide people (for example, field headquarters versus main headquarters).

- A leader shows favoritism to his or her former division (or to any loyalty beyond the team).

Move beyond factions. Factionalism can destroy everything a team works for. As a leader, you need to learn how to recognize factions, understand their sources and causes, and do whatever is in your power to eliminate them or reduce their negative power. Manage yourself carefully so you do not seem to be giving undue attention to any one special group. The key to handling and re-uniting factions is to be objective, just, and fair in all dealings with the factions and the whole team.

Tip: Tips for Dissolving Factions

- Create redistributed subteams that force people to work together.
- Remove people's focus from the boundaries that divide them and remind them of the boundary that encircles them.
- Take action to balance power within the team.
- Reexamine reward systems.

"Scapegoating is worse than an individual with an attitude problem. I have zero tolerance for scapegoating. That's about as anti-team as you can get. Talk to people collectively as a group. If that's how they're deriving their power, you really have to zap it. You just put your foot down, 'Here's what I know. I don't want to hear excuses. This is going to stop.'"

—Jeanne Weldon

Step between one-on-one conflicts

All forms of noncreative conflicts, hostility among team members, dissension, and resistance can disrupt or even destroy the team's work. Be alert for every type of disturbance in the personal relationships between team members.

Beware of bullies and scapegoats. If one member bullies another person or the rest of the team into accepting his viewpoint, the team

Steps for Resolving a Personal Conflict

1. Identify the conflict. It may not be immediately obvious, but you'll soon feel the hostility. The two people may be avoiding one another or criticizing each other openly during meetings or privately to you or other team members. Pay attention to their body language and the tone of their voices when they do interact.

2. Do fact-finding separately with each person. Listen and observe carefully and objectively. Seek the root of the conflict.

3. After listening to each person, bring the two parties together and try to mediate a solution. Have team members identify their conflicting perspectives as alternative scenarios and develop them. Give each scenario its due time and respect. Have each person look at those same possible outcomes and arrive at an objective conclusion. You may want to ask another team member to assist in the mediation.

4. At the end of the mediation, you, as the leader, need to explain the consequences if the problem behavior continues.

5. If the mediation is successful, misunderstandings can be eliminated and the conflict resolved or, at least, reduced.

6. If the mediation is not successful because the problem lies in some unresolvable realm such as a personality clash, then you may have to establish a special set of ground rules to control each person's behavior and avoid having their conflict infect the rest of the team.

7. If even ground rules won't resolve the negative effects of the conflict, you may have to take more severe steps and remove or replace one or both of the parties.

members will resent both the bully and the decision. Just as one member can be a bully, another member can become a scapegoat. When a few or all of the team members oppose or refuse to listen to one member's ideas, you are losing the value of the stifled member as well as the cooperation of the team.

When bullies or scapegoats emerge on your team, intervene promptly. During meetings, quiet the bully and reassure the scapegoat. Remind the team of the original ground rules that everyone's voice must be heard and respected. Encourage members to find some common ground or new possibilities.

Confront individual conflict. Even an ongoing conflict between two people can harm a team's morale. This problem is somewhat more complex than a difficult single person. However, once again, it's your job to confront the conflict and resolve it in some way that does not jeopardize the team goals.

"It's very hard to not choose sides in an internal conflict. You could assume both people are equally to blame, but chances are it's not the case and it's probably more one than the other. I think ultimately what it comes down to is that you let the people know that the team's goals are at risk and if they can't get along, one of them is going to have to leave."
—Jeanne Weldon

Reinvigorate commitment

Whether or not your team has problems as it moves along in the process, periodically plan to reinvigorate their commitment.

Revisit the team's goals regularly. Make sure the team's goals remain consistent with those of the larger organization—and keep senior management informed about major developments.

Work with the team to break goals down into specific tasks, and set a timetable for completing them. Don't be overly optimistic: having false expectations about what you can accomplish will only set you and your team up for failure. But don't underestimate what the team can accomplish either. By expecting too little, you're wasting the team's potential.

If your workload has grown or your goals have changed, the original plan may no longer be valid. Be realistic about what the team can actually accomplish in a given time period—then, alter your expectations. Be sure to communicate these changes and the reasons for them to everyone involved—team members, senior management, and any other stakeholders.

Reward your team. Teams, like individuals, are motivated by rewards. A carefully designed reward system can be an important driver of your team's success. In creating the reward system, be sure to

- emphasize the group, not the individuals

- offer rewards not only at the end of a project but also at strategic milestones

- consider carefully who should give out the rewards

- decide what to do about members who leave or join the team mid-project.

Tip: Tips for Reinvigorating Commitment

- Maintain a "learned optimism." Take five minutes at the beginning of each meeting to highlight what has already been accomplished and where you're headed.
- Remind team members of the various individual benefits that will result from successful team performance.
- Identify "small wins," simple tasks that can help a team maintain its confidence and morale.
- Remind members of the significance of their work.

Tip: Tips for Rewarding Hard Work Well Done

- Give lunches, mugs, t-shirts, and so on.
- Order a subscription to a professional publication for everyone on the team.
- Delegate an important presentation or a fun trip to a team member so he can shine, have a good time, or get a chance to develop professionally.
- Reward people with opportunities for their own professional growth and development.
- Promote the person out of your team—even if its difficult for you!

"I always tried to promote people. When you get a good team, you move people to jobs they want more. It's always been a hard thing for me when someone terrific wants to move up, but you absolutely have to support that because if they're good for the team you built, then they're going to be good for another team. Promoting people is important to the team. It builds trust that you're looking out for them, and more importantly, it's human."

—Jeanne Weldon

Use creative reward systems. There are many ways to reward team accomplishments beyond just paying them money. Figure out what kinds of rewards will be meaningful to the team as a whole. Be creative. Make the rewards fit the spirit of the team. For example,

- announce team accomplishments at larger, organizational meetings, and to senior management

- ask team members to serve as consultants to other teams

- place notes in the personnel files of individual team members

- send the team a handwritten personal note in recognition of a task well done

- empower the team with greater freedom and authority to make decisions.

The most important reward you can give is ongoing positive feedback. Acknowledge your team's accomplishments at team meetings. When positive feedback comes from outside the team—for example, a letter from a satisfied customer or kudos from a client—share the praise with everyone. After all, they've earned it. And when receiving recognition yourself, always give credit to the team.

What You COULD Do.

Let's go back to Derek's problem.

The mentor suggests this solution:

This is a really tough situation. As the leader, Derek has to go into that next meeting ready to perform. He could try to do something funny but relevant, such as wearing a cap of the local underdog sports team. He has to get his team's competitive juices flowing. He should really play on the underdog theme, and, at the same time, remind them of their past successes.

How to Evaluate
Performance

In evaluating team performance, attaining the team's goals is, of course, critical. So too is the way in which the team achieves those results. If you have been monitoring the team's performance and processes regularly, there will be fewer surprises at the end.

Use appropriate performance measures

Teams can identify a set of specific performance measures that can be used to chart their progress toward their goals. While the type of measures used depends largely on the specific work of the team, the following list provides samples of the types of measures often used:

- achievement of business goals for which the team is responsible

- customer satisfaction

- actual cost of production compared to budgeted costs

- quality of product or service

- profits

- delivery time

- downtime in hours

Factors in evaluating performance. Traditional performance evaluation is most often oriented toward results or output. The primary difference in evaluating team performance is that, while results are still critical, the way in which the team achieves those results is also important. The collaborative process used to achieve results is an important measure of team performance. Given that, the performance factors listed below are divided into two equally important categories: results and process.

Results factors:

- achievement of team goals

- customer satisfaction

- quantity of work completed

- job knowledge and skills acquired

Process factors:

- support of team process and commitment to the team

- level of participation and leadership

- collaboration

- conflict resolution

- planning and goal setting

- participative, win-win decision making

- problem solving and application of analytical skills

- level of credibility and trust

- adherence to agreed-upon processes and procedures

- building and sustaining interpersonal relationships

- willingness to change and take risks

- individual and team learning

Select evaluation methods

There are many different approaches available for measuring your team's success. They vary widely in complexity, cost, and time required. You should consider a more elaborate method for a team whose mission is extensive and will have a significant impact on organizational performance; for teams with narrower missions, simpler methods can still provide a great deal of learning. The methods include

- benchmarking against other similar teams in similar organizations

- evaluating the team's progress against original goals and schedules

- observation of the team by an outside consultant

- encouraging regular, informal team discussions to assess the team's functioning

- project debriefing sessions to identify what did and did not go well and how this learning can help future projects.

Review the performance of individual team members

An individual team member actually performs a number of roles—for example, as an individual contributor, as a member of the team, and as a member of the larger organization. Thus, in reviewing performance, it is helpful to combine at least a couple of the following methods to address performance in each of those roles:

- **Peer rating.** Team members assess each other's contributions.

- **Customer satisfaction rating.** Internal and external customers rate the performance of the team and of the individual members.

- **Self-appraisal.** Each team member rates his or her own performance.

- **Team leader review.** You, as the team leader or the supervisor, evaluate each individual's performance.

- **Management review.** Department heads or managers of the team leaders evaluate individual and team performance.

Reward your team

Evaluations help reinforce team strengths and identify areas for improvement. When team evaluations are linked to appropriate, creative rewards, your team is motivated to achieve both progress and process results.

Tips and Tools

Tools for
Leading a Team

Worksheet for Forming a Team

Team Purpose

Expected Activities

Intended Results

Available Resources

Constraints

Necessary Skills and Qualities

Expected Team Members

Extent of Decision-Making Authority (for example, Recommend or Implement)

Duration

Checklist for Assessing Your Team's Goals

Use the checklist below to assess characteristics of your team's goals.

Question	Yes	No
1. Did the team jointly create its goals?		
2. Has the team translated its purpose into specific and measurable performance goals (for example, "Respond to all customers within 24 hours")?		
3. Are they team goals rather than organizational goals or just one person's goals (for example, yours)?		
4. Does meeting the goals require the contribution of every team member?		
5. Are the goals clear?		
6. Are the goals simple?		
7. Are the goals realistic?		
8. Are the goals ambitious?		
9. Can the goals be measured? *If the goals cannot be measured, can you and your colleagues determine when you have achieved them?*		
10. Do the goals measure the team's cross-functional purpose?		
11. Do all team members agree with the way in which the goals will be measured?		
12. Do the goals provide clear yardsticks for team accountability?		
13. Are the team's goals prioritized?		
14. Is the priority of those goals clear to and agreed-upon by all team members?		
15. Do all team members understand the goals?		
16. Do all team members explain the goals in the same way?		
17. Do all team members agree with the goals?		
18. Do the goals allow for small wins along the way?		
19. Do these small wins or benchmarks reflect critical points in the path toward the team's goals?		
20. Do the goals add real value to the company's results?		
A highly effective team is likely to answer "yes" to most or all of these questions. If you answered "no" to any of these questions, the team may want to discuss the issue and how it may be affecting the team. Changing or refining the team's goals may lead to better performance.		

Team Contact Information

Use this form to record each team member's contact information,
including how and when he or she prefers to be reached.

TEAM MEMBER:			Role:
Mailing Address:			**E-Mail:**
Office Phone Number	**Home Phone Number**	**Fax Number**	**Best Time to Call**

TEAM MEMBER:			Role:
Mailing Address:			**E-Mail:**
Office Phone Number	**Home Phone Number**	**Fax Number**	**Best Time to Call**

TEAM MEMBER:			Role:
Mailing Address:			**E-Mail:**
Office Phone Number	**Home Phone Number**	**Fax Number**	**Best Time to Call**

TEAM MEMBER:			Role:
Mailing Address:			**E-Mail:**
Office Phone Number	**Home Phone Number**	**Fax Number**	**Best Time to Call**

TEAM MEMBER:			Role:
Mailing Address:			**E-Mail:**
Office Phone Number	**Home Phone Number**	**FaxNumber**	**Best Time to Call**

Role Clarification Worksheet

Ask each team member to complete the worksheet. Responses can be compared as part of a team discussion about roles.

1. List roles/responsibilities of each team member:

Team Member Name	Roles/Responsibilities

2. Roles or specific areas of responsibility that are unclear:

Aspects of my role that are unclear:

Aspects of others' roles that are unclear:

3. Roles that overlap or conflict:

4. Roles that should be shared within the team:

5. Additional roles or responsibilities that should be assumed by the team:

Promoting Team Interdependence

Answer the checklist questions to see how well you are currently promoting team interdependence.
Generate specific information that you can use to promote team interdependence.

Checklist: How Consistently Are You Promoting Team Interdependence?	Yes	No
1. Is it clear how members' individual work and the team's work are equally important to the team's success?		
2. Do member's individual goals coincide with the team's goals?		
3. Have you spoken to the team and described how each individual's ideas and skills are vital to the team's success?		
4. Is the team aware of which specific skills each team member brings to the team?		
5. Do you remind individual members how their skills contribute to the team's success?		
6. Do you encourage the team to take responsibility as a team for its actions?		
7. When an issue arises, do you encourage the team to work together to come up with solutions?		
8. When the team chooses a course of action, do you encourage all members to accept the action (no matter where the idea originated)?		

If you answered "no" to any question, complete the worksheet questions that follow and consider when and how in the coming weeks you can focus more consciously on building team interdependence.

Ways to intertwine your goals and the team's goals:

Individuals to remind of their importance to the team's success:

Upcoming activities where you can encourage team responsibility:

Team problem-solving and collaboration skills to develop:

Team Time-Out: How Are We Doing?

Use this time-out audit periodically to gather information from each team member to create a group profile the team can use as a focal point for a discussion about, "How well are we doing as a team?" The discussion provides an opportunity to compare points of view objectively, and if need be, to get back on track and move forward more productively.
Each team member can complete the time-out audit. Individual responses should be kept confidential. Compile the individual responses into a group profile for the team to share in a team meeting.

Team Name: **Date:**

Team Goals/Team Purpose:

Rate your opinion of the team's effectiveness on the dimensions listed below, with "1" representing an ineffective area in need of improvement and "5" representing an area of effectiveness and strength.

Aspect/Dimension	Rating					Comments/Example
	1	2	3	4	5	
Goals/purpose						
Meetings						
Ground rules and norms						
Communication						
Leadership (designated or rotating leadership)						
Workload/distribution of work						
Energy/commitment level						
Resources (availability/adequacy)						
Management of stress						
Decision making						
Respect for differences/diversity						
Management of conflict						
Level of participation/inclusion						

Comments:

The biggest challenge we face as a team is:

Our greatest strength as a team is:

The one thing I would most like to see the team do is:

Checklist for Evaluating Yourself as a Team Leader

To evaluate yourself as a team leader, answer these questions. Your answers will help to pinpoint areas of improvement that may lead to better leadership.

Question	Always	Often	Rarely	Never
1. Do you facilitate effective team decision making?				
2. Do you work with the team to determine work assignments?				
3. Do you help the team evaluate itself?				
4. Do you ensure that the team is accountable for its work?				
5. Do you do "real work" beyond decision making, delegating, and agenda setting?				
6. Do you put team results ahead of personal achievement?				
7. Are you able to strike a balance between doing things yourself and letting other people do them?				
8. Do you promote constructive conflict?				
9. Do you help the team resolve conflicts and problems in a positive and constructive way?				
10. Do you widen your perspective to help the team clarify its purpose, goals, and approach?				
11. Do you avoid actions that unnecessarily limit team members?				
12. Do you constantly challenge the team to sharpen its common purpose, goals, and approach?				
13. Do you build trust in team members by acting in concert with the team and its purpose?				
14. Do you create opportunities for team members, sometimes at your own expense?				
15. Do you explain the team's purpose and act to promote and share responsibility for it?				
16. Do you think about and describe your role in team terms instead of in individual or hierarchical terms?				
17. Are you a champion for the team? For example, do you fight for the resources that the team needs, promote the team's best interests in dealings with the company, and have an undying belief in the project?				
18. Do you identify and act to remove barriers for the team?				
19. Do you accept team failures rather than blaming other people?				
20. Do you accept performance shortfalls and find solutions to address them, rather than excusing them by pointing to things outside of your control?				
21. Does your attitude reflect dependence on the team?				
22. Do you see when your actions could hinder the team?				
23. Do you believe that you do not have all the answers?				
24. Are you able to give up command and control to help the team perform better?				
25. Are you able to change your leadership style as the team develops?				
26. Do you wholeheartedly believe in the team's purpose and in the people on the team?				
27. Are you able to strike a balance between too much control and too little guidance?				
28. Are you able to strike a balance between making tough decisions and letting others make them?				
29. Are you patient while the team talks about its purpose, goals, and approach?				
30. Do you encourage team members to take risks needed for growth and development?				
31. Do you challenge team members by shifting work assignments so that the same members are not always responsible for the same types of work?				
32. Do you challenge team members by shifting role patterns so that the same members are not always assuming the same types of roles?				

The leader of a highly effective team is likely to answer "always" or "often" to most of these questions. If you answered "rarely" or "never" to any questions, you might want to think about the issue that the question implies and about ways in which you might be inhibiting team performance.

Working through a Disagreement

Use this worksheet to diagnose a disagreement among team members and to plan a discussion about how to "get unstuck."

Describe the disagreement.

Diagnose the disagreement. *(Who is involved in the disagreement? What's the underlying cause? What's at stake for these team members?)*

Team Member	What's at Stake for This Team Member?
1.	1.
2.	2.
3.	3.

What's at stake here for you?

What setting will you use for the discussion?

Script a discussion about the disagreement. *(What do you plan to say? How might others respond?)*

What You Plan to Say	How Others May Respond
1.	1.
2.	2.
3.	3.

Generate alternative solutions. *(Team members should have an opportunity to offer possible solutions first. Generate a dialogue to explore solutions and why the topic is important.)*

Solutions	How/Why This Solution Adds Value
1.	1.
2.	2.
3.	3.

Keep reminding all those involved that we are on the same team. *Try to find win-win solutions.*

Test Yourself

Test Yourself offers 10 multiple-choice questions to help you identify your baseline knowledge of leading a team.

Answers to the questions are given at the end of the test.

1. Which of the following phrases does NOT belong in a description of a *team?* "A team is a small number of individuals with _____"

a. Complementary skills committed to a common purpose.

b. Similar skills and background.

c. Common performance goals.

d. An approach for which they hold themselves collectively accountable.

2. Understanding how much authority the team truly has is critical. Which of these aspects generally does NOT reside solely within the scope of team authority?

a. Resource decisions within budget.

b. Design of the approach to the project.

c. Evaluation of the team's ongoing progress.

d. Changes in the team's schedule or deliverables.

3. What are the two leading causes of a failed team?

    a. Inadequate resources to get the work done and inadequate reward systems.

    b. A team focus limited to tasks and ignoring internal relationships.

    c. Lack of management support and weak leadership.

    d. Irresponsible team members and team members uncomfortable with the process.

4. When a team's tasks are complex and require specific skills, what's the suggested optimal team size?

    a. A small team of 5 to 9 members.

    b. Minimum of 12 to 15 members, to ensure that all of the required skill sets are present.

    c. Up to a maximum of 25 people.

5. Four frequently used decision-making approaches for making team decisions are (1) majority rule, (2) consensus, (3) small group decision making, and (4) leader decides with input. Which of these is most likely to help build team commitment?

    a. Majority rule and consensus.

    b. Only consensus.

    c. Small group decision making and majority rule.

    d. Leader decides with input.

6. Which of the choices most accurately completes this sentence? "Being a team leader is like being _____."

    a. A coach; you help and support team members to encourage their best performance.

    b. A traditional manager; you must focus on ensuring that the team's tasks are completed on time and on budget.

    c. A quarterback; you carry the ball but need the team to work with you.

7. Early into a project, you notice a clique forming within the team. You consider reassigning members of the clique to work closely with other members. Is this a good idea?

    a. No.

    b. No, not unless all other efforts to get the clique apart fail.

    c. Yes.

8. Before removing an individual who is not a "team player" from the team, should you consider bringing him before the team for a group discussion?

    a. No, this is never appropriate.

    b. Yes, this is appropriate after you have worked to resolve the issues with the individual.

    c. Yes, the recommended first step is to bring the issue to the team.

9. Your team is stuck mid-project, and it's up to you to help them get unstuck. Which of these actions is NOT a viable choice to help the team get back on track?

   a. Lead a team discussion to revisit the team's purpose, approach, and goals; probe for differences in opinion and resolve them.

   b. Establish a common immediate goal and achieve it.

   c. Bring in new information and different perspectives from within the organization to explore or compare the situation with other situations.

   d. Change the composition of the team's membership.

10. Traditional performance evaluation is most often oriented toward results or output. What is a primary difference in evaluating team performance?

   a. The entire group is evaluated on performance, not each individual.

   b. How the team collaborated is evaluated as well as the result.

   c. You as team leader are evaluated as well as the outcome or result.

Answers to test questions

1, a. By building a team that includes a range of knowledge, expertise, and perspectives, a manager can generate more creativity and effectiveness than can be found in a single individual or in a group with similar skills.

2, d. In general, upper management generally does get involved in decisions such as changes in the team's schedule or deliverables. Other instances of upper management involvement might include decisions about expenses over a given budget amount, changes in key product suppliers or service providers, whether or not to bring in outside resources, or changes in companywide policies or goals.

3, c. Lack of management support and weak leadership are the most frequent reasons that teams fail. However, all of the choices shown might cause a team to fail.

4, a. Although the optimal size for a team clearly depends on the team's goals and tasks, in general, small teams (5 to 9 members) tend to be most effective when the team's tasks are complex and require specific skills. Larger teams (up to 25 people) can be effective if the tasks are simple and straightforward and team members agree to delegate tasks to subgroups as needed.

5, a. In selecting a decision-making approach, your team must weigh some trade-offs. The more involved the team members are in the decision-making process, the more likely it is that they will support the outcome. As a result, the consensus and majority rule approaches can help build team commitment.

6, a. Team leaders are more like coaches. In moving from a traditional management role to that of team leader, you shift the focus toward facilitating rather than directing and rely on the expertise of others rather than serving as the "expert." As a team leader, you initiate actions and processes, model team behavior and serve as a counselor, mentor, and tutor for team members.

7, c. Teamwork means the entire team, not the work of a few select people. You need to discourage cliques within your team. Reassigning members to work closely with other members can help them get to know one another better.

8, b. First you need to make the difficult member aware of his actions, listen and discuss the issues, and give him a chance to change. If no change occurs, bringing the individual before the group is appropriate. At this meeting, it is critical to stay on the issues and not to allow personality conflicts to become the focus.

9, d. Yes, that's the choice that is NOT a viable solution for a team that is stuck. Teams get stuck mid-project for a variety of reasons. At times, members' sense of direction may weaken; there may be insufficient or unequal commitment to team performance; critical skill gaps may emerge; the team may encounter confusion, hostility, or indifference from other groups. Your role, as a facilitator, is to help the team find and articulate—and resolve—whatever the issue may be.

10, b. The primary difference in evaluating team performance is that, while results are still critical, the way in which the team achieves those results is also important. The collaborative process used to achieve results is an important measure of team performance.

To Learn More

Notes and Articles

Pablo Cardona and Paddy Miller. "The Art of Creating and Sustaining Winning Teams." Harvard Business School Note. Boston: Harvard Business School Publishing, 2000.

> This guide reveals the secret behind winning teams. First, the authors define what a team is, distinguishing it from other kinds of work groups. Second, they show what characteristics team members need to form a winning team. Next come the stages of team development and the basic processes teams must master at each stage. Finally, you learn how to build team commitment and performance.

Rob Cross. "Looking Before You Leap: Assessing the Jump to Teams in Knowledge-Based Work." *Business Horizons,* September 2000.

> Teams often seem a natural and easy solution for improving collaboration and productivity in knowledge-based organizations. But the transition to teams can be difficult.

Anne Donnellon. "Listen To Teams." *Insights,* Summer 1996.

This article examines what can be learned by listening to teams and examining how they communicate.

Loren Gary. "Managing a Team vs. Managing the Individuals on a Team." *Harvard Management Update,* March 1997.

Managing a team is not the same thing as managing the individuals who make up the team. To maximize team effectiveness, ask four questions: (1) Is a team the best organizational structure for this effort? (2) Have I established collective goals that the team members can make their own? (3) What signals am I sending to members about how the team should interact? (4) Does my performance management system actually reward interdependence and mutual accountability?

Harvard Business School Publishing. "Handling Conflict in Teams." *Harvard Management Communication Letter,* April 2000.

Interpersonal conflicts are common in today's team environment. This article offers powerful tips for recognizing and dealing with difficult personality types on your team.

Harvard Business School Publishing. "Why Some Teams Succeed and So Many Don't." *Harvard Management Update,* January 2000.

Teams—sometimes they have great results, and sometimes they are huge failures. What makes the difference? Research shows that it's how teams are managed—and whether your company as a whole really supports teamwork.

Jon R. Katzenbach and Douglas K. Smith. "The Discipline of Teams." *Harvard Business Review* OnPoint Enhanced Edition. Boston: Harvard Business School Publishing, July 2000.

> The essence of a team is shared commitment. Without it, groups perform as individuals; with it, they become a unit of collective performance. A working group relies on the individual contributions of its members for group performance. But a team strives for something greater than its members could achieve individually.

Jim Kling. "Tension in Teams." *Harvard Management Communication Letter,* July 2000.

> Conflict is inevitable in teams, and it is often seen as difficult and uncomfortable. Most people try to avoid conflict altogether, but that can cause problems in the long run. Instead, some experts suggest using team conflict to encourage creative solutions. For this to work, team leaders need to set ground rules such as confronting conflict directly and not allowing it to get personal. A team leader's own behavior is crucial to directing the behavior of the team.

Christopher Meyer. "How the Right Measures Help Teams Excel." *Harvard Business Review,* May–June 1994.

> Senior managers play an important role in helping teams develop performance measures by dictating strategic goals, ensuring that each team understands how it fits into those goals, and training a team to devise its own measures.

Books

Anne Donnellon. *Team Talk: The Power of Language in Team Dynamics.* Boston: Harvard Business School Press, 1996.

> Donnellon argues that the gap between the ideal and the reality of team work is due to the failure to recognize and address the paradoxes that teamwork poses for individuals, teams, managers, and organizations. The central paradox is that a team requires both the preservation of differences among its members as well as the integration of those differences into a single working unit. The way team members talk reflects and shapes the way they resolve these tensions.

Deborah L. Duarte and Nancy Tennant Snyder. *Mastering Virtual Teams: Strategies, Tools, and Techniques That Succeed.* New York: Jossey-Bass, 2000.

> Designed for those who work in—as well as lead—virtual teams, this book is divided into sections that focus on their unique inherent complexities, their creation, and their operation. Real-life examples and the authors' experienced observations are complemented by an abundance of helpful checklists and practical exercises.

Deborah Harrington-Mackin. *Keeping the Team Going: A Tool Kit to Renew and Refuel Your Workplace Teams.* New York: AMACOM, 1996.

> This book describes how to get teams through a mid-life crisis. Topics covered include getting a team back on track, reen-

ergizing teams, building strategic relationships, building trust, resolving conflicts, problem solving and decision making, and measuring a team's worth.

Harvard Business School Publishing. *The Art of Managing Effective Teams. Harvard Management Update* Collection. Boston: Harvard Business School Publishing, 1999.

> This comprehensive collection from the editors of the *Harvard Management Update* newsletter provides you with all the expert ideas, insights, and solutions you need to help your teams succeed.

Harvard Business School Publishing. *Making Teams Work. Harvard Business Review* Collection. Boston: Harvard Business School Publishing, 1996.

> What is a team? And when should you assemble a team to handle a project or other effort? How can you ensure your team's success? This *Harvard Business Review* collection offers guidelines for assembling management teams, creating cross-functional teams, motivating and measuring a team's work, and more.

Steven D. Jones, Michael M. Beyerlein, and Jack J. Phillips, eds. *In Action: Developing High-Performance Work Teams.* Vols. 1–2. Alexandria, VA: American Society for Training & Development, nd.

> The authors provide case studies showing a variety of approaches to implementing teams in the workplace. They examine team configurations such as virtual teams,

empowered teams, joint-venture teams, and self-managed teams. Includes guidelines for moving from supervisor to team manager.

Jon R. Katzenbach, ed. T*he Work of Teams.* Boston: Harvard Business School Press, 1998.

Managers are seizing on teamwork as an easy solution for meeting aggressive goals, only to meet with frustration when their teams prove difficult to predict and control. Katzenbach gathers together articles from the *Harvard Business Review* that address the challenges and rewards that await every successful team.

Jon R. Katzenbach and Douglas K. Smith. *The Wisdom of Teams: Creating the High-Performance Organization.* Boston: Harvard Business School Press, 1993.

The authors believe that many business leaders have a tendency to overlook opportunities to employ the tremendous potential of teams for improving organizational performance. The authors provide insight into the differentiators of team performance, where and how teams work best, and how to enhance team effectiveness.

Sources for
Leading Teams

We would like to acknowledge the sources that aided in developing this topic.

Terrell Buckley, New England Patriots defensive back.

Anne Donnellon, Associate Professor in the Management Division, Babson College, Wellesley, Massachusetts.

Scott Ferguson, Boys Varsity Soccer Coach, Brookline High School.

Timothy O'Meara, Director of Technical Services, Ameritech Indiana.

Steve Sullivan, Vice President for Communications, Liberty Mutual Group.

Richard Tait, former software developer at Microsoft and co-founder of Cranium, a successful board game company.

Jeanne Weldon, Event Planner and former Catering & Conventions manager, Sheraton Boston.

Julie Bick. "Inside the Smartest Little Company in America." *Inc. Magazine,* January 2002.

Pablo Cardona and Paddy Miller. "The Art of Creating and Sustaining Winning Teams." Harvard Business School Note. Boston: Harvard Business School Publishing, 2000.

Anne Donnellon. "Listen to Teams." *Insights,* Summer 1996.

Anne Donnellon. *Team Talk: The Power of Language in Team Dynamics.* Boston: Harvard Business School Press, 1996.

Deborah Harrington-Mackin. *Keeping the Team Going.* New York: American Management Association, 1996.

Gordon Edes, "Head Games." *Boston Globe,* 2 February 2002.

Loren Gary. "Managing a Team vs. Managing the Individuals on a Team." *Harvard Management Update,* March 1997.

Jon R. Katzenbach and Douglas K. Smith. *The Wisdom of Teams: Creating the High-Performance Organization.* Boston: Harvard Business School Press, 1993.

Jim Kling. "Tension in Teams." *Harvard Management Communication Letter,* July 2000.

Robert B. Maddux. *Team Building: An Exercise in Leadership.* Menlo Park, CA: Crisp Publications, 1992.

Don Mankin, Susan G. Cohen, and Tora K. Bikson. *Teams and Technology: Fulfilling the Promise of the New Organization.* Boston: Harvard Business School Press, 1996.

"Tech Information." *Inc Magazine,* January 2002.

Richard S. Wellins, Dick Schaff, and Kathy Harper Shomo. *Succeeding with Teams: 101 Tips That Really Work.* New York: Lakewood Publications, 1994.

Notes

Notes

Notes

Notes

Notes

Notes

Notes

Notes

Notes

Notes

Notes

Notes

Notes

Notes

Notes

How to Order

Harvard Business School Press publications are available world-wide from your local bookseller or online retailer.

You can also call:
1-800-668-6780

Our product consultants are available to help you 8:00 a.m.—6:00 p.m., Monday–Friday, Eastern Time. Outside the U.S. and Canada, call: 617-783-7450.

Please call about special discounts for quantities greater than ten.

You can order online at:
www.HBSPress.org